TRIUMPH HOUSE
Poetry with a Purpose

NEW PERCEPTIONS

Edited by

CHRIS WALTON

First published in Great Britain in 1998 by
TRIUMPH HOUSE
1-2 Wainman Road, Woodston,
Peterborough, PE2 7BU
Telephone (01733) 230749

All Rights Reserved

Copyright Contributors 1998

HB ISBN 1 86161 481 0
SB ISBN 1 86161 486 1

FOREWORD

For many years poetry has always played a minor part in the lives and education of young people. Many youngsters found it boring and showed little interest. But over the years there has been more poetic material to study and not just the traditional and complex poems written by the likes of Tennyson and Wordsworth.

Today many youngsters enjoy writing poetry, allowing them to show their creative potential, whilst at the same time exercising their imagination. Teachers now encourage pupils to write poetry more often, and together we now have a new generation voicing their opinions and thoughts on many topical issues which affect people everywhere.

New Perceptions is a collection of poetry written by youngsters under the age of 16. As they demonstrate their literary skill in wonderful style, the young authors give their opinions and views on what 'girls and boys' really think of each other and how they perceive the world for the future to be. The result is a truly enjoyable collection of poems to be read time and time again.

Chris Walton
Editor

Contents

A Solitary Citizen	Gemma Steele	1
Floreen	Katie Burt	2
Global Destruction	Carmen Light	3
The End	Laura Godwin	4
The World To Come	Kay Ma	5
A Lesson In Love	Chloe Shoniwa	6
A Disaster	Natacha Leopold	7
A Vision Of Him	Nicola Taylor	8
Double Trouble	Louise Montgomery	9
Girls On Boys	Carys Jones	10
Girls On Boys	Naomi Ankrah	11
Caroline	Gary Ward	12
A World For The Future	Rebecca Carter	13
Unstoppable	Emma Reece	14
Home Again To A Planet Of Harmony	Kuljeet Kaur Panesar	15
Boys	Kerry Morfett	16
Boys, Yuck!	Rebecca Duriez	17
Girls On Boys, Boys On Girls	Melissa Rudderham	18
Big Night Out	Vikki Powles	19
Lads!	Aimee MacKay and Sarah Paxton	20
A Teenage Boy Freak	Phoebe Okoli	21
Girls On Boys	Vanessa Long	22
Why Are Boys So Immature?	Kay Lister	23
In The Absence Of Love	Lauren Andrews	24
Boys, Boys, Boys	Liliana Marchese	25
Boys On Girls	Stefan Kaminski	26
Boys	Selina Marks	27
Boys And Girls	Sheila Silveira	28
Girls On Boys	Hayley Flynn	29
Girls On Boys	Kelly Alderdice	30
Boys' Rules	Gina Millward	31
My Ex-Boyfriend	Helen Thacker	32
Boys And Baths!	Jennifer Bull	33
Girls On Boys	Rebecca Hallgate	34

Boys	Melissa Livingstone	35
Relationships	Fiona McAllister	36
Boys On Girls	Mark McGill	38
Boys	Katrina Norton	39
My Thoughts On Boys	Lydia Carter	40
Girls	Adam Stewart	41
Boys	Leah Walsh	42
A World For The Future	Laura Harrison	43
What A Wonderful World	Catherine Kerr	44
A World Without?	Jenny Farrell	46
Our Future World	Gemma Dawson	47
A World Of The Future	Thomas Huggins	48
A World In The Future	James Evans	49
Girls	Shaun Ryan	50
Boys On Girls	James Crabb	51
Men Are Pants	Laura Acreman	52
I Will Be There	Bhinder Chopra	53
The Beastly Boys	Cassie Harvey-Smith	54
Girls/Boys	Kelly Davies	55
The Future At A Glance	Paul Carey Jr	56
The Disappearing Future	Vicki Bonner	57
Truth Be Told	Sarah Levene	58
They're Hurting Me!	Emma-Jane Welsh	59
A World For The Future	Dorothy Howard	60
A World For The Future	Leanne Gibbons	62
The Day Out!	Sera-Jean Glover	63
A World For The Future	Leanne Symes	64
Once	Nishani Balendra	65
A Different World	Terrie McKenna	66
A Whole New World	Natasha Raheen	67
A World For The Future	Heather Kelly	68
World For The Future	Jessica Jacques	69
A World For The Future	Emma Madigan	70
The World	Abbey Hewitt	71
A World For The Future	Sonia Sangha	72
The Future Of The World	Hannah Murphy	73
The Last Everything	Stefanie Elrick	74
The Earth	Erin Bryson	75

Title	Author	Page
A World For The Future	Nicole Bruton	76
A World For The Future	Imran Khan	77
Do You Know?	David Fisher	78
The Rainforest	Charlette Hinds	79
A World For The Future	Afshan Badshah	80
A World For the Future	Oliver Lee	81
The Future	Kitty Isaac	82
Neither Good Nor Bad	Helen Withington	83
A Waste Of Time	Laura Eastwood	84
What's So Different About Girls	Antony Longmire	85
Girls Vs Boys	Shelley Wood	86
Girls I Don't Know Why	Anthony Driver	87
Boys On Girls	Simon Adams	88
Girls On Boys!	Annika Holliland	89
A World For The Future	Sukhveer Bhaker	90
Our Future	Letty Lamdin	91
A World For The Future	Emma Swift	92
Pairair The Future	Sarah Morris	93
Children In Conflict	Michael Godwin	94
Future Of Pollution	Jennifer Rickard	95
Technology Time-Bomb	Lindsay Hudson	96
Stop	Rachel Laming	97
Likes	James Bunning	98
Untitled	Naomi Connor	99
Boys Will Be Boys	Rachel Burbridge	100
Men, Boys, Idiots	Fiona Patterson	101
Boys	Gemma Keith	102
Girls On Boys	Claire Hancock	103
Boys Have No Brains	Holly Barton	104
Girls On Boys	Hannah Osborn	105
Boys	Karina Heslewood	106
Girls On Boys	Caroline Ayres	107
What Will There Be?	Abigail Watkins	108
Earth	Ffion Haf Hughes	109
The World	Louisa Gibb	110
No Me . . . No You	Zoe Mitchell	111
A World For The Future	Emma Deakin	112

Title	Author	Page
Hold On	Victoria Whewell	113
Boys	Cally Fitzsimmons	114
Walk On By	Michael McQueen	115
Nin 1901-1996	Michelle McDonald	116
Why?	Amanda Hampson	118
A World For The Future	Claire Nicole Pomphrett	119
Today Was Not	Marie Simpson	120
A World For The Future	Amy Lawrence	121
A World For The Future	Lauren C Argent	122
Boys, Boys And More Boys!	Emma Freeman	123
I Don't Know How	Sharon Arnold	124
He's The Only One For Me	Tanya Bailey	125
A World For The Future	Rob Lean	126
The Turning Of The Century	Vicki Hancock-Ekberg	127
A World For The Future	Christopher Thompstone	128
A World For The Future	Annabel Stevenson	129
A World For The Future	Michael Connolly	130
Here Comes The Millennium	Paul Chandler	131
The Right Road	Nicola Farrer	132
Tomorrow	Lizzie Harvey	133
The Morning Of Tomorrow	Tine Berg	134
A World For The Future	Zoë Thompson	135
A World For The Future	Catherine Phillips	136
A World For The Future	Faye Willicott	137
Our World In The Future	Charlotte Marshall	138

A SOLITARY CITIZEN

Who is this woman?
I see sitting
on a bench, wrapped up in a coat?
Why, does she just sit there?
And look all around? So melancholy;
So solitary, with no-one to talk to
cut off from the rest, a sad face
just sits there, sits there all day
doesn't move or utter a word,
No-one, upon no-one, knows who she is,
The vagrant that sits there, on the bench
In the middle of the dirty street.

No money lines her pockets,
No food does she eat.
Her days are long and drawn out and,
For someone who has been a victim of loss
can do nothing, but wait,
For her time to come.

Gemma Steele (12)

FLOREEN

When people say 'I'm starving,'
They don't know what they mean,
They may be a little hungry,
But not as hungry as Floreen.

She lives in South Africa,
Alone, no-one's there.
There's no food for miles,
And water is rare.

Soon she will come to death,
Abandoned by her mother,
Who died of starvation,
Along with her brother.

When people say 'I'm starving,'
They don't know what they mean,
They may be a little hungry,
But not as hungry as Floreen.

Katie Burt

GLOBAL DESTRUCTION

The earth lies still, motionless serenity,
A former land of goodness, of love and of divinity,
Now suspends itself shamefully in eternal darkness,
The sun became an enemy, the future became timeless.

Where once the playful breezes blew amidst religious life,
The weather cycles buried now, as if the hallowed light,
That shone upon God's children as they played throughout the lands,
Bathing in majestic seas and praying in the sand.

Benevolence and amity bound the seven seas,
Civilisation was harmonious and our Creator rested pleased,
With the racial interaction and equality for all,
With the freedom, faith and fraternity He had attempted to install.

But as this honourable world revolved, His subjects did observe,
That they were domineering and supreme upon this earth,
Glutted with conceit of this, they revelled in themselves,
Naive that underneath them await the infernal depths of Hell.

So selfish, idle and savage did these barbarians become,
That the candles remained unlit, the hymns remained unsung,
The men devoured each other, stole their souls and ran away,
As the devil's perpetual darkness asphyxiated day.

From His celestial position in the ever-blackening sky,
He peered upon the mockery of His glorious structure of life,
He sent a cataclysmic bolt to extinguish all the sin,
The red tides stung humanity, the world then ceased to spin.

Now the earth lie still, motionless serenity,
A former land of goodness, of love and of divinity,
Now suspends itself shamefully in eternal darkness,
The sun is now an enemy, the future is now timeless.

Carmen Light (14)

THE END

God had created our unique world,
but we had destroyed it,
We had poisoned the air that once was clean
and made it a deadly gas, which,
was in turn going to kill all life.
We had hunted all creatures
until there were none left.
The dying forests lay silent,
there were now no tigers' paws upon the dead soil.
Where beautiful, snow-capped mountains used to lie,
now lay mountains of our greedy waste.
Houses now lay as rubble,
the smoke and ashes had penetrated into the morbid sky.
We had torn out the silver stars
and blacked out the sun.
Day had died, been wrapped up in the darkness.
Night had engulfed the Earth.
Our once beautiful, clear oceans
had been washed away.
All that remained of Human life,
were the untouched footprints upon the dry, untouched soil
and the destruction we had left to rot away,
as no fresh wind came to blow the scars away.

Laura Godwin (14)

THE WORLD TO COME

I can see . . .
The world to come.

Computers are all we need,
Machines rule the earth.
Mankind is a mere small seed,
In our place of birth.

You can see . . .
The world to come.

You no longer need me,
I no longer need you,
Nobody needs anybody,
There's no more needing to do.

Who can see,
The world to come?
Not me, not you, not anyone.

All hope of perfect future,
Is a desperate illusion.
All I can see is pollution,
What was once a place of glory,
Is now a sad ending story.

I can see,
The world to come.
I can see . . .
Death.

Kay Ma (14)

A Lesson In Love

He looked at me,
I looked at him,
He winked my way,
So I gave him a grin.
I batted my eyelashes,
He flicked his hair,
For flirting,
He had a natural flair.
As he walked past,
He brushed at my side,
I imagined myself,
As his blushing bride.
I thought of a date,
With the man of my dreams,
But he had other ideas,
Or so it seemed.
He passed me a note,
'Not to offend'
But he wanted the phone number,
Of my very best friend.

Chloe Shoniwa

A Disaster

A shirt that was once white now brown and half-undone,
                                              tie loosened and hair scruffy.
His shoes kicked off at the entrance as he makes
                                              his way to his territory.
His smelly feet are mounted on the table, TV remote at hand.

The loud sounds of commentators and spectators followed by a joyous
                                            scream of *goal!* Invade my thoughts.
All peace and quiet is snatched away from the home,
                                            selfish in my opinion.

Travelling only to drain the kitchen of all its supplies.
Countless numbers of goals fill the evening's atmosphere.
Now he's fast asleep on the couch, saliva sipping from the corner of
                                                                his mouth.

Feet still up, hands clutching a large bag of crisps, Coke spilt all over
the table, socks and shoes in the same position as they were before and
                                                                   TV still on.

A disaster in its own right.

Natacha Leopold (14)

A Vision Of Him

There's a rainbow in your smile;
That reflects my every gain,
That calls me close to you,
After heartache's morning rain.

There's sunrise in your hair,
That reflects every curl,
Your touch an enigma,
Like a wonder within my world.

There's magic in your eyes,
That calls without words,
Of whispers in the willows,
That no-one else has heard.

There's a shiver in your lips,
That warms the smallest chill,
Of winter's harsh touch,
That awaits your kiss still.

You're a step too far away,
For you to love me too,
And with each lonesome day,
I'll forever search for you.

And there's a small lonely owl,
That with night hears a silent cry,
And the time has come, I know,
For I must say goodbye.

If you pass hear my heart say,
I'm sorry it's sad, yet true,
I wish I had the words,
For now I know, I love you.

Nicola Taylor

DOUBLE TROUBLE

The two I have in mind are my brothers.
I wouldn't swap them for any others.
They may annoy me for most of the day,
But I still wouldn't want them to go away.

To make things worse they're identical twins,
So in arguments guess who wins?
One can pretend that he is the other
But they can't yet trick my father and mother.

They fight and scrap and argue daily
But I know they like each other really.
I know for a fact that they have no taste.
They support Liverpool - what a waste!

I think I know why I like them at the minute:
'Cause when I'm at our house they're not in it.
I'd miss them if they were not here,
But just for now I'll steer well clear.

Louise Montgomery (14)

GIRLS ON BOYS

Everyone knows that the female of the species is more deadly than the male,
And that hell hath no fury as a woman scorned.
But in a world where the females have become dominant,
What happens to the male with his dominating streak?
It's common knowledge that man is possessive,
This is shown in early years of puberty,
When men are boys,
Boys need girls but in their pride they'd never admit it,
Behind every big man there's a big woman,
Males have evolved into three distinctive categories,
The lager lout who drinks himself to an early grave,
Or smokes so many cigarettes that his middle name is Benson and Hedges,
The rich bachelor who woos his women with his wealth and excessive spending,
He has a steady job which females look for as it gives them security in later years,
Then there is the tall, dark and handsome male,
Every woman's dream with his good looks and gentlemanly manners,
But he is always too good to be true with some dark secret just waiting to be unleashed,
Girls today become women much sooner than past generations,
They take on responsibility at a very early age,
Our society is home to hundreds of teenage mums,
So if you asked girls what they think of boys you'd have different responses from different people.
I personally would say:
It's a woman's world and man's just there for the ride.

Carys Jones

GIRLS ON BOYS

They may be clueless,
They may stink.
But they can help you understand
how boys think.
They laugh stupid laughs,
and tell stupid tales,
about how they stole a bus
in a remote town in Wales.
They annoy you so much
You want to rip out your hair.
They won't leave you alone
even though you're crying out in despair.
All they talk about is girls, cars and school.
If they see a girl they like
they just stand there and drool.
But they have their good points too,
Like for 1 . . .?
and 2 . . .?
OK so they don't have any
but I've thought about it and I have found
boys are great to have around.

Naomi Ankrah (15)

CAROLINE

One word can make me smile now,
or two if you know who I mean,
I'd love to offer her my innocence,
I don't need it anymore.

This evening has closed her eyes,
now she's dreaming of someone I don't know,
I wonder if this trespass is welcome,
I could slip inside and find out.

Left her wandering on a Thursday
- not a very happy Thursday
I had to leave for what seemed like forever,
but it's so good to be back with the old crowd.

This morning has opened her eyes,
such a beautiful day, she just had to,
I wonder if I go I'd be welcome,
I could slip inside and ask her.

I could not live without her
the question is, could she live with me?
I asked her once and she said that she could,
now evening closes our eyes together.

Gary Ward (17)

A World For The Future

It's the year 2050,
And I'm looking back down the years,
Wondering why we destroyed our planet,
It makes me break down in tears.

Only fifty years ago,
I was happy and young.
All my friends were alive and well,
Our days were full of fun.

There was peace in Europe,
And we breathed fresh air.
We even drank clean water,
Oh, it's just not fair.

There was plenty of countryside,
And animals roamed free.
Vegetation was plentiful,
How careless could we be?

We've destroyed the ozone layer,
And made the ice-caps melt.
Many lives have been lost,
And much pain felt.

Please think about what you're doing,
And what could happen to you.
If we keep neglecting our special world,
Then this poem may come true.

Rebecca Carter (14)

UNSTOPPABLE

It glints murderously,
 Deadly as nightshade,
  Villainously choking the fish,
   It's unstoppable.

 It vigorously executes the sea creatures,
  As evil as the devil,
   Polluting the sea and ocean,
    It's unstoppable.

 It stealthily murders the sea birds,
  Powerfully killing everything in its wake,
   As cunning as the fox,
    It's unstoppable,

        It's oil.

Emma Reece

HOME AGAIN TO A PLANET OF HARMONY?

Home again to a planet of harmony . . .
But as the fog cleared and the truth appeared,
All there was to see were the painful wounds
of Mother Earth.
They were poisoned with pollution,
and pale with exhaustion for the plants and
trees are being destroyed.
They are saddened by the agony that animals
are being put through,
Some of whom had lost the fight to stay
alive safe away from the humans
altogether.
Home again to a planet of harmony?
With pollution from vehicles, nuclear
explosions, wastage, polluting our oceans
and seas?
Very likely I think not.
When shall we learn?
There seems to be no turning back,
But if we all are serious and determined to
help our world we can.
For the wounds on Mother Nature are
forever waiting to be helped to heal.
A plea from Mother Nature.

Kuljeet Kaur Panesar (12)

Boys!

Boys here,
Boys there,
Boys are everywhere,
They're up my nose,
And in my hair,
Boys are everywhere.

Kerry Morfett

BOYS, YUCK!

Boys, boys, are silly things,
Boys, boys, always scare us,
Boys, boys, are noisy things,
Boys, boys are hairy.
Boys, boys, horrible things,
Boys, boys, make us sick.

Rebecca Duriez (9)

GIRLS ON BOYS, BOYS ON GIRLS

So boys can kick a football
And boys can tell a lie,
But could they put on make-up?
I'd like to see them try!

Some boys can give you right grief,
And it winds you up no end,
So shout them some sexy comments
It'll drive them round the bend.

They also have this image
And are always in a fight,
They answer back at teachers
Now what gives them the right?

Boys generally think they're funny
And roll around in the dirt,
But the thing that annoys me most of all
Is when they try to lift up your skirt!

Some boys can be very sweet
And pamper you which is rare,
Others want to meet your family
As if they'd actually dare!

But boys are also sexist
And like to be in control,
They seem to think they're just the best
When they've scored a goal!

So some you love, some you hate,
And some you just want to kill,
Just remember when you're out to dinner
Both! Should pay the bill.

Melissa Rudderham (15)

BIG NIGHT OUT

I'm going out tonight
With the boy of my dreams
All the girls like him
Well, that's what they scream!

I'm standing at the chippy
It's turned ten o'clock
He's thirty minutes late
Have I been stood up?

He finally comes smartly dressed
Adidas jumper and jeans neatly pressed
He turns girls' heads as he walks down the street
But I know that it's me he's come to meet.

Hand in hand, walking in the park
On my neck he leaves his mark
We've been out for ages now
Then he says he has to go
Jumps on a cloud
And away he floats
See you tomorrow,
Same place, same time.

Can dreams come true?

Vikki Powles (14)

LADS!

You get big heads
and think you're cool
When you strut
around the school.

Every time we see you
you're wearing the same
You're getting yourselves
a very bad name.

You have spots and great big blackheads
Those double-lensed glasses
And your hairy legs.
The names you call us are really sad
But really you're not all that bad.

Aimee MacKay & Sarah Paxton (15)

A Teenage Boy Freak

When I was six, I played with toys
I never, never, played with boys.
Their grubby knees, their greasy hair,
Their dirty clothes with wear and tear.
They always would spit and swear,
Whatever they did, they just didn't care.

The years have passed,
My views have changed,
And now that I am sweet sixteen
It's finally crystal-clear to me,
How gorgeous sexy boys can be.

Their sparkling smiles,
Their strong physique
Which makes my knees go soft and weak
Their loving arms, the sweetest kiss
That fills me with eternal bliss.

And when they whisper *'I love you'*
Those words, they make my heart go blue.
I could not have it any other way
Thank goodness boys are here to stay.

Phoebe Okoli

GIRLS ON BOYS

Confidence bashers,
Losers, just cruel,
Want to be noticed,
In trouble at school.

Immature noises,
Laughter and grunts,
They get away with,
The filthiest stunts.

If you are different,
They'll get to you, call -
Pick on a weak point,
And make you feel small.

It does not work,
Don't let them win,
They take advantage,
Of weakened skin.

You are no sheep,
So do not follow,
You will become,
Empty and hollow . . .

Vanessa Long (14)

WHY ARE BOYS SO IMMATURE?

Why are boys so immature?
You wear the wrong trainers and they think you're poor
You wear your hair in a plait
And they just hate that.
You're called a swot if you're good all the time
If you buy something cool, they shout 'That's mine!'
If you ask someone out
They blab the news about.
They pull your bobbles out
And won't give them back until the teacher shouts.
If you try to look smart
They call you a tart.
If you slip on the path
They just stand there and laugh.
They throw rubbers everywhere
If they hit you they just don't care.
They yank at your skirt
In winter they put snow down your shirt.
Boys always fight
They think they are always right.
You're called a nerd if you enjoy school
If you hate school you're called cool.
In tests boys always do poor
Why are they so immature?

Kay Lister (12)

IN THE ABSENCE OF LOVE

In the absence of love I
write letters poems see people animals walk talk be merry lead a life
But there is a lacking

I am
touched spoken to asked told reasoned with pacified abused laughed at

In the absence of love I can still
breathe have friends make friends buy food go shopping to the cinema
behave normally
but still I feel unwanted

I want to be
seen noticed thought about flirted with gazed at phoned written to
kissed held touched in a special way argued with in a lover's tiff

In the absence of love.

Lauren Andrews (14)

Boys, Boys, Boys

Some boys have dark skin
Some are fair
Some have black, brown, red and blond hair,
Some are tall and short
Some wear trousers
Some wear shorts
Some have specs, freckles and pimples.
Some have a laughing mark, which is a dimple.
Some have clean, dirty or crooked teeth, usually
        in the bathroom for one hour at least.
Some think they are fit and cool, one look
at them they think you will drool.
Some think they are big and tough, showing
        off doing their stuff.
Some will never change, because they
        never act their age.

Liliana Marchese (13)

BOYS ON GIRLS

Girls are annoying
Girls are fussy
Girls act smart
Girls are bossy.

Girls are naughty
Girls can be nice
But girls are not
All sugar and spice.

My girlfriend is shy, funny, happy
and means everything to me.

Stefan Kaminski (12)

BOYS

There is a boy in my class who makes my heart beat really fast,
His eyes are blue his hair is brown,
He's just the nicest boy around,
He's really nice, kind and great,
He asked me out on a date,
We went down town and looked around,
We ate our lunch he walked me home,
Then I told him he had to phone,
It was late and time went by,
Then he phoned and made me cry,
I ran to my room,
Then slammed the door,
Boys who needs them?
Not me, that's for sure.

Selina Marks (12)

BOYS AND GIRLS

Boys are famous for being strong and bold,
But *girls* have to put up with them when they're old.

'*We* try to show *them* our lovely curls . . . but they don't care,
Do they, *girls*?'

They wear make-up till they look like clowns,
Then try to impress *us* by giving us strange frowns.

Boys play football all day . . .
They don't even let *us* play!

Girls make *us* play with dolls,
'I wonder what's wrong w'it *them* after all . . .'

But at the end of the day *we all* get on . . . probably 'cause no one likes to be alone . . .

In their own . . .

Sheila Silveira (12)

GIRLS ON BOYS

Lads love to keep you in suspense
They are such fickle creatures
One minute they love you to bits
The next they'll crack jokes about your features

Even so, they make great friends
They've got a bad side and a good
Deep down they really do care
Which any normal person should

I think they are outgoing
With them I have a laugh
It is possible to be just mates
Without being their other half

We both are equal
And should give each other chances
But there are certain things
That, still, only man sees.

Hayley Flynn (14)

GIRLS ON BOYS

Boys can be silly,
Yet boys can be sweet.
Young boys will always,
Race up your street,
Shooting some hoops,
Playing some ball.
Scraping their knees,
Climbing a wall.

Boys can be cool,
But boys can be weird.
Some boys in gangs,
By the nation, are feared!
But boys can be super,
Boys can be great.
Others torture insects,
Sealing their fate.

Older boys are stupid,
Acting so fine.
All having fights, saying,
'That girl is mine!'
Their looks are pure evil,
I'm glad looks can't kill!
Joyriding, thieving,
Evading the Bill.

But boys can be lovely,
Boys can be kind.
Some boys will always,
Be in *my* mind!
A boyfriend, a friend, a brother, a dad.
Without these boys, my life would be sad!

Kelly Alderdice (14)

BOYS' RULES

Boys think they are way too hard to have emotions,
All they think about is girls' boobs and bums,
Footie comes first in their eyes,
No boy cries,
Smiling is pretty uncool,
Boys think cool is drinking and going to play pool,
It's OK to be nice to girls, as long as
              no one sees them doing it.

Gina Millward (14)

MY EX-BOYFRIEND

There was a time you made me feel I could fly,
But you broke my heart and you made me cry,
I thought that I'd just break down and die,
You said you loved me but that was a lie.

You soothed my pain, you calmed my stress,
But then you dumped me and made my world a mess,
I thought you loved me, I thought you were the best,
Now I look at it in perspective, you're no better than the rest.

We used to work as one, but then you split us into two,
You thought you understood me, but you haven't got a clue,
We always used to be 'us', now we're simply me and you,
Now you've got the nerve to say, you want to start anew.

You asked me for an answer, 'Yes' you think I'll say,
Well here's my final answer - 'Absolutely not, no way!'

Helen Thacker (15)

BOYS AND BATHS!

Boys!
Who understands them and do they understand
themselves?
They understand football but definitely not
baths!

When they are running around the playground
and they start to smell,
They don't care, they smell anywhere,
Especially when they're sitting next to you
in class!

They go home and sit in front of the TV
They think they are cool, but really
they drool,
And they are horrible and smelly!

Boys and baths definitely don't mix!

Jennifer Bull (12)

GIRLS ON BOYS

When girls have a boyfriend,
This is what they feel,
It's so unreal.

You're weird,
Yet fun, but sometimes say things wrong.
You sometimes let me down,
or even make me frown.
You send me round the bend,
but you are my boyfriend,
and when we have a tiff,
I ask myself this . . .

Who would I rather hang around with?
I know the answer,
         It's boys!

Rebecca Hallgate (13)

BOYS

In this world there are boys,
Who always make so much noise.
They're here to make your life hell,
Just when things are going well.

They like to pretend they're a man,
Doing the best, they can.
But when things start to go wrong,
They don't hang around for too long.

Boys like to think they're really tough,
And no one compared to them is too rough.
They think they're the strongest man ever,
When really they couldn't knock over a feather.

Plus out of their ass,
Comes a whole load of gas.
Which you could set on fire,
Then they say it wasn't me. What a liar.

Boys drive you up the wall,
Because all they do is, play football.
They say us girls are a pest,
When really us girls are the best.

Melissa Livingstone (15)

RELATIONSHIPS

There's always going to be people I like and people I don't,
I don't have to get on with everyone I meet, in fact I know I won't.
I meet boys I want to have as my mates,
And others I want to go out with on dates.
But if my boyfriend breaks up with me getting over him can take years,
Is he really worth all these mixed emotions and tears?
He might be the one who makes me feel like inside me I've got
butterflies,
I spend ages getting ready for him and I always let out these dreamy
little sighs.

He's stood me up before and if he does it again I'll end up crying,
He doesn't call me for days and inside I feel like dying.
Then, everything seems like a dream, me and him holding hands,
walking through the park,
I stay with him all day but I have to go home when it's dark.
But then everything becomes so confusing,
I have to decide if things are 'winning' between us or 'losing'.
At night will it be *his* kiss I want so much,
And will I lie awake missing his soft gentle touch?

Maybe I'll lie awake because I feel so hurt,
It might end up that he spends the days slagging me off and treating
me like dirt,
Then I ask myself 'Is this the guy I find full of romance?'
If he is he'd better show me soon or he'll be on his last chance,
This guy I love so much has been so deceiving. I can feel it, he's
going to break my heart,
So should I forget about him, try and find someone else and make a
brand-new start?

Before I decide I have to ask myself would I do anything for this guy?
Does he brighten up my life, care about me and love me?
Does he make as many of my dreams come true as he can?
Whenever I see him does he take my breath away and steal my heart?

Well, on the whole I think guys are great to have around,
So if you're lucky enough to have the man of your dreams found,
then hold on to him and love him *forever!*

Fiona McAllister (12)

BOYS ON GIRLS

Boys think girls
are lovely

Boys think girls need
more attention

Boys think girls
have more common-sense

Boys think girls
are beautiful

Boys think girls
are just right

Mark McGill

BOYS

Boys I hate so,
Every inch from head to toe.
Boys are always mean to me,
When I play football can't you see.
They're from outer space,
They think everything's a race.
They're such show-offs,
They irritate me like coughs.

Katrina Norton (11)

MY THOUGHTS ON BOYS

When I think of boys,
I think of the immature type,
The macho, hard man type,
The male teenage stereotype.

But if I think more carefully,
They're not all like that,
They're not all anything,
They're all individuals.

If I think more carefully still,
I guess they're quite like girls,
Some funny, some serious,
Some fat, some thin.

When I think about it,
Boys can be anything,
Girls can be anything,
Boys and girls are just genders,
They don't tell you about the person.

Lydia Carter (13)

GIRLS

Big girls, small girls,
very very fat girls.
Tall girls, short girls,
very very small girls.
Black hair, brown hair,
ginger or blonde hair.
Good girls, bad girls,
very very sad girls.
Long hair, short hair,
very very thick hair.
Some girls smile, some girls sigh,
But the other girls always *cry!*

Adam Stewart (12)

BOYS

Boys are the scruffiest things you've seen,
Especially their bedrooms, they're never clean.
Dirty clothes cover the floor,
As the day goes by there's more and more.
Smelly socks in with all the clothes,
If they're clean or dirty, no one knows.
Mouldy cheese on stale bread,
        has been left for days under the bed.

Leah Walsh (12)

A World For The Future

What will our world be like in the future?
Will it be dirty and full of unhappiness?
With animals dying, and plants as well
With people all glum and sad as can be.

What will our world be like in the future?
Will it be clean and full of happiness?
With so many animals we cannot count
With plants growing day by day
With people who are happy and never glum.

What will our world be like in the future?
Will it be combined with dirt and cleanliness?
Will it be colourful and dull as well?
Will there be many animals or not enough?
Will people be happy and sad as well?

What will our world be like in the future?

Laura Harrison (12)

WHAT A WONDERFUL WORLD

'Look at my beautiful world,'
Cried God from above.
'Why isn't anybody showing
Their peace and their love?'

He looked all over England,
Then He looked at Spain.
He checked the whole world,
And then He checked again.

God saw the rubbish,
That had been thrown around,
He saw all the mess
That was lying on the ground.

'Stop,' cried God,
'Oh help the world I made.
It is looking terrible,
Can it be saved?'

God punished the ones,
Who spoilt the land
And gathered the good ones
In His hand.

God told people
They must understand,
That He made the world
With His own gentle hand.

And that they
Must learn to care,
To be kind and gentle
And to always share

Their peace and love so
God can look down from above
And think *what a wonderful world.*

Catherine Kerr (10)

A World Without?

A world without flowers
A world without trees
A world without summer
No whispering breeze
A world without thoughts
A world without dreams
A world without poetry
A world without streams
If we didn't have a future
If we didn't have a past
What would we look forward to
As the years slip past?

Jenny Farrell (10)

OUR FUTURE WORLD

This planet is ours to share
People act as if they don't care
If we don't start to help and pitch in
This world will end up in the bin.

Just little things like recycle a can
Will do no end of good for man
Pollution spoils our streets and roads
Soon wildlife will be gone even frogs and toads.

If everyone began to learn
Then maybe the tables we could turn
We could keep this environment a pleasant place to live
If people would stop taking and give.

We all live in this world together
We shouldn't drop litter not even a feather
If we don't begin to see
There will be nothing left for you or me.

Gemma Dawson (14)

A World Of The Future

I've always thought about the 'world in the future',
New inventions or maybe a new creature.
Lots of things to do and see,
Maybe a robot version of me.

A big question and a big solution,
We probably would have stopped pollution.
The latest bike or hover car,
Maybe you can change what creature you are.

Everything works by solar beams,
New home entertainment machines.
We shall all die in 2000 some say,
but no-one knows what's yet to come.

Thomas Huggins (12)

A World In The Future

The new world looks like
It has been hurled.
Cracks in the ground,
Aliens that are never found.

We see hover cars
And laser guns,
From afar.
But the Creator was just,
Having fun.

Here we are,
Looking around in frustration,
When aliens are building a battle station.
But then I see a river,
Which makes me shiver.

And near the end of time
Of the futuristic world
We are building bridges,
From one planet to the next.
But as we play around
On the planet we found,
And made,
Some aliens are planning
A crusade.

And I finish off my story
With not much going for me.
Apart from the futuristic world,
Which is to be
You will see . . . !

James Evans (12)

GIRLS

Girls are spiteful,
Especially to each other,
Some end up crying,
Home to their mother.

Girls do well in their exams,
They are always hopeful,
When they're happy at the end,
Mothers look delightful.

Girls are very nice,
To a decent lad,
Well, that's what I find,
And I'm very glad.

Girls want us to be clean,
They want us to wear good threads,
When we're having a game of footie,
They must be off their heads!

Girls try to look nice,
To impress a boy,
But what they don't know is,
We treat them as a toy.

Girls are really nice,
I'm not trying to put them down,
They try to get all dolled up,
And look just like a clown.

Girls ask us to the cinema,
They expect us to pay,
They eat loads of popcorn,
What more can I say?

Shaun Ryan (13)

BOYS ON GIRLS

Girls are putrid and sad
and sometimes they treat me
like Sir Galahad,
But girls themselves think
they're nice
and precise
But really they're rude
and moody
like a cat in a hat.
All they do is buy shoes
and booze
and like flashing their boobs
when they're out on the loose.

James Crabb (13)

MEN ARE PANTS
*(They don't just wear them,
They are them!)*

It's not that I don't like you,
I care for you, I truly do,
But I've got my eyes on better things,
So, can we just be friends?

I'm flattered that you asked me out
You must be very brave
I couldn't have got the courage up
But, can we just be friends?

Do you really think I'd go for you?
You're really not my type
I'm sorry if I hurt you but,
Can we just be friends?

It's kind of a statutory phrase
When letting someone down
It is meant in the nicest way and
Can we just be friends?

Laura Acreman (16)

I Will Be There

When old age comes upon you,
With your beauty gone down,
All your lovers have left you,
All on your own,
I shall still be there for you,
To love and to care,
No matter what happens,
I shall always be there.

You probably don't need me now,
Your beauty is great,
You have many after you,
Asking for a date.
I just sit there - a flower's seed,
Waiting to blossom with your love's need.
Laughing from the outside,
And crying from within,
Waiting for the day,
When your heart I shall win.

Bhinder Chopra

THE BEASTLY BOYS

Punching, fighting, spitting,
'Man United rule!'
Kicking, throwing, hitting,
'No, Arsenal are cool!'

Shoving in the corridors
And running in the hall.
'I do exist as well you know,
Or don't you care at all?'

Punching, fighting, spitting,
'Get out of the way!'
Kicking, throwing hitting,
'Don't care what you say.'

Fighting every playtime,
For the girls in heels,
Staring at them fixedly,
Ruining school meals.

Punching, fighting, spitting,
Dad says it's a game,
Kicking, throwing, hitting,
We like them, all the same.

Cassie Harvey-Smith (11)

GIRLS/BOYS

Some boys are alright
But others are tight
And you feel like saying 'Get out of my sight'
Then they shout at you with an awkward tone
And you feel like you're trapped in a zone
Some boys are shy
And don't even wave goodbye.
Some boys are rude
And think they are dudes
Some boys are pushy
But others like eating sushi
Then there's the slob
Who should go get a job
But there's always someone out there for you
But which one to choose
'Cause I don't want to lose out
I just want to get
       out and about.

Kelly Davies (12)

The Future At A Glance

In the future we shall have robots who clean
and dust our house, who get rid of and exterminate
every rat and mouse.

In the future there will be computers who
teach us English and maths, who order in the shopping,
and even run us baths.

In the future there will be people who have nothing to do,
because computers and robots will even clean the loo

I wonder what the future has in hand for you,
you may be used for experiments in London Zoo

Paul Carey Jnr (12)

THE DISAPPEARING FUTURE

In an African rainforest, so far away,
Steam rises everywhere with trickles of rain.
Men with chain saws will find their way,
And will soon cut the forest away.

Hot and steaming like an enormous greenhouse,
26°C and 60 inches of rain.
As the trees grow tall with a frightful fear,
The trees and wildlife will soon disappear.

We need the rainforest to breathe in air,
People and animals also live there.
Just think, what have they ever done to us?
Don't you think this has gone far enough?

Why not recycle? This is the way.
Instead, we're chopping the forest away.
When we're breathing in the air,
Just think life in the rainforest is so unfair.

Don't you think this should all stop?
Stop our earth from becoming a concrete block.
If the rainforest did come to an end,
Just think, it will take many lifetimes to mend.

Vicki Bonner (14)

TRUTH BE TOLD

Truth be told -
The world is old,
The moon is silver,
The sun is gold.
Things are bought
And things are sold . . .
They come and go,
Let truth be told.

Truth be told
That life is rolled
Around one
Egotistic mould,
But every corner
Can still fold
And spoil perfection,
Truth be told.

Truth be told -
We've grown too bold,
The night is long,
The days are cold . . .
There's nothing left
For man to hold.
The world is dying . . .
Truth be told!

Sarah Levene (13)

THEY'RE HURTING ME!

I am the old tree
Where the bird makes its nest,
Where the insects live,
And the squirrels rest.
But I'm no longer smiling.
I wear only a frown,
For the humans have come
And they're cutting me down.
Their axes are sharp,
But they just cannot see,
That with every strike
They're hurting me!
They think I don't matter.
I'm just an object to chop,
But I'm alive and I'm hurting
And I wish they would stop.

Emma-Jane Welsh (16)

A World For The Future

Here we are a million years on from when the cavemen lived,
Computers, cars and intercoms never really did exist.

Now we are here we might as well admit how much the world has changed,
It really has progressed a bit and it is changing now.

Already we've a taste of the year 2000 with the Millennium Dome,
One thing known across the land is about computers shutting down.

There will be flying buses and flying cars in 2030,
Jam won't be sold in jars but in small plastic boxes.

No one will eat cans of beans or a portion of chips,
Everyone will survive it seems on vitamin pills for breakfast, lunch and tea.

One good thing is that there will be no schools at all anywhere
All the written work we do will disappear -
Yippee, except we'll have to type it and E-mail to a teacher.

Marks and Spencer and New Look will gradually disappear before our very eyes,
No one will pick up or read a good book because it will be on the Internet.

This might happen but what I'd like to see is nothing at all like this,
I want the future planet to be a caring, giving and loving place.

I want to see the poor people and the bereaved able to survive on their own,
Their burdens lifted, their debts relieved and their grudges taken away.

All the countries that are now at war to let their fighting cease,
To stop the bombing and the shooting, for them to make an agreement for peace.

The animals also play a part. I want to see less cruelty towards them,
They are living too,
They have a brain, feelings and a heart, they can understand like us.

Whether these things really come true it's difficult to know,
I hope the things that I want people like me to do turn out
just like I plan.

Dorothy Howard (12)

A World For The Future

My world for the future,
Flowers bloom everywhere.
Putting daffodils in our hair,
Seeing things grow here and there.

Baby lambs prance about,
Children jump and shout.
Chicks hatch here and there,
They pick the daffodils out of our hair.

Leanne Gibbons (11)

THE DAY OUT!

The sun is scorching
It's burning a hole
The sand is hot
It's burning like coal

The people are busy
Getting ready to go out
They're packing their bags
Everybody's out and about

Everybody's happy
Nobody's feeling sad
The children are all laughing
The grumpy man is mad

Everybody stopped
They all start to listen
There it is again
The sky starts to glisten

It's starting to rain
Everybody's taking cover
A little girl starts to cry
And so does her mother

The day is ruined
Everyone's sad
The day turned out
To be nothing but bad.

Sera-Jean Glover (12)

A World For The Future

The world of the future
Will be an unhappy place,
With atom bombs and nuclear waste,
An overwhelming surge of greenhouse gas.

The world of the future
will it exist?
Can we humans start to resist
An overwhelming urge to destroy the world?

Perhaps in the future we shall be
But a collection of fossils in history,
Or maybe we shall all look the same,
A clone of Hitler, that would be a shame!

All speak the same language,
Wear the same clothes,
Have that silly moustache under our nose,
And never leave that cage of monotony.

The world of the future
Will be torture and pain,
Unless we give up our stupid game -
Destroying the future.

As we sit here and ruin the world,
We destroy the future for those unborn,
Is it fair to sit here and watch and wait
While the future is destroyed?

The world of the future
Will be extinct
Before it has started.

Leanne Symes (13)

ONCE

There was a time to live
There was a time to die,
But all we seem to do now is cry,
There was a time of trees,
And a clean ocean breeze,
But pollution has destroyed the environment
Despite our desperate pleas.
There was a time when life was ruled by love,
But money is now far above,
And happiness seems so hard to find
With the world filled with people most unkind,
Where lifeless technology plays the main role
And Man's inventions will take control,
Emotions will soon be a thing of the past
Where wealth will rule and love will come last.

Nishani Balendra (15)

A Different World

All different colours of plants.
All different types of ants.
It can be fun
Just looking at one.
All these midges and fleas.
Chestnut, plum and apple trees.
All these amazing creatures
With all their tiny features.
There is such a place as *Animal Kingdom*
Where all the animals have their freedom.

Terrie McKenna (12)

A Whole New World

The world I want for the future,
Is a world of peaceful harmony;
Where a person shouldn't be judged by their colour,
For colour is only skin-deep;
A place where different religions,
Respect each other's beliefs;
Where arguments can be settled by compromising
instead of killings and war;
A world where stealing and murder do not
exist anymore;
Where drugs aren't needed for pleasure
because they aren't worth what they cause;
Poverty is no longer a worry we all have good
standards to live for.
Greed and people striving for power, is just
a part of our past;
A world where everyone is equal and opportunities
are open for all.
A world where we don't abuse the earth,
But we love it and protect it each day;
The pollution to our environment is over
and finished for good;
Cruelty to animals has come to a stop,
the red light is here to stay;
Animals are now free to live,
we let them have back their life.

This is the world I want for the future;
A perfect, sincere world;
A world where love is the formula;
Some day we'll have this world.

Natasha Raheem (14)

A World For The Future

There's a lot that could happen for our world of the future.
There are lots of good things and bad things.
There are lots of world leaders who don't really care,
Who just muck around and play with their hair.
They paint grass green so it looks good, I think that
our world of the future is going to be a mess if
they don't do something.

We won't go forward into high-tech computers,
we'll go downwards, where there is no grass, just mud.
Where there are no flats just slums.
Where there's no rules just people in poverty.
We won't grow to be a better place if we don't
all join together and help the earth to be a better place
for the world of the future.

Heather Kelly (12)

WORLD FOR THE FUTURE

The world is a spherical scene,
Wrapped up in a blanket of blue and green.
Inside this blanket are many emotions,
Many thoughts and feelings,
Locked deep inside our human skin.
We are only one of the many species,
Which inhabit our earth,
And we vary from me to you,
Some think of only themselves,
While others think of more than one,
Should this change?
Should we all look out for each other?
Look out for the environment, plants and wildlife,
Stop the killing and the spraying,
Think of our world and its future,
Should it end,
Like it started,
With one big *bang?*

Jessica Jacques (13)

A World For The Future

In came the bulldozers,
and down came the trees.
The oxygen level's slipping,
then out came the bees.
Animals are dying,
and their homes destroyed.
No one cares, they think it's funny.
Only if they get their money.
The air is filled with harmful gases
People get ill in great masses.
So shall we live to see tomorrow
Or be made to suffer in the years that follow?

Emma Madigan (13)

THE WORLD

Why can't they see they're polluting me?
Why can't they see they're destroying me?
Why can't they see I'm dying?

Abbey Hewitt (12)

A World For The Future

It's time to put a stop to all
The anguish and the pain,
An end to all the trees that fall
From which we make no gain.

The choking fumes that smother us
Are danger in disguise.
Now's the time to make all the fuss,
Time to open your eyes.

Don't wait to see wildlife dying.
Picture them in your heart,
Their tearful eyes simply crying,
Come on, let's make a start!

Make ignorant people aware.
Why? Some may care to say.
It's your task to teach them to care,
To help our world today.

Oil slicks, smoke and radiation
And the nuclear waste,
Cause disease and suffocation
Take less time and make haste!

Peace and love, we can still provide
By taking a firm stand.
No need to run, no need to hide,
We'll unite, hand in hand.

Put an end to all pollution,
The problem's grown too wide.
There is only one solution,
All working side by side.

Sonia Sangha

THE FUTURE OF THE WORLD

The future of the world is in our hands,
We have the power, we're in command,
But why do people suffer and feel pain?
Why do people fight? Are they insane?

The future of the world is in our hands,
We have the power, we're in command,
But why is the rainforest about to disappear?
Why do the native tribes have fear?

The future of the world is in our hands,
We have the power, we're in command,
But why do people take what isn't theirs?
Do they think, or is life just a dare?

The future of the world is in our hands,
We have the power, we're in command,
But why are we living in a polluted place?
Why may this be a catastrophe that ends
                              the human race?

We need a new approach to this,
We must try to get along in harmony and bliss,
We need to change this world and fast,
Otherwise this world will be the last.

Hannah Murphy (12)

The Last Everything

'What's the matter Mum?' the little girl asks,
'Nothing much, just another species gone.'
'Which one this time?'
'Sheep.'

What will the world be like, when everything that nature
provided is turned to metal?
What will happen when all oxygen is sold in cylinders,
And the food you eat is not really food,
It's just a carbon copy of what food once was?
What will happen when you have to pay to see grass,
In a little glass box,
Surrounded by strobe lights and chains?
Just imagine the pain there would be,
When you couldn't go outside for a breath of fresh air,
Because all the air is gone,
And radiation levels are dangerously high,
So high that you'd die instantly, an instant being one half of a
second.
You'd switch on your TV,
And witness the destruction of another animal,
As the men in charge try to find a way out of the mess they
have created.
But everyone knows there isn't a way,
Everyone knows, and some are relieved,
For which world would you rather live in?
The one that we now are beginning to create,
Or a world where there is nothing to trouble you, and nothing
can die again anyway.

Stefanie Elrick

THE EARTH

Our time on this earth
Is not very long
But that doesn't stop us
We've made the earth a bomb!

                        Putting deadly gases
                        In the air
                        But some people say
                        'We don't care!'

But in twenty years
When the earth is worse
We'll realise then
That we are the curse.

                        When our children are dying
                        And the earth is dead
                        We'll remember then
                        What we said.

'We don't care.
The earth belongs to everyone.'
But now we have ruined it
For our daughters and sons.

                        Take care of the earth
                        It is the only one we've got
                        Please listen to me
                        Don't let the earth go to rot!

Erin Bryson (13)

A World For The Future

They come in all sorts
Of different shapes,
Sizes.
They are green,
Slimy and smell repulsive.
These aliens we are talking about
Are *litter bugs*.
Soon they will rule.
Help!

Nicole Bruton (13)

A World For The Future

All the time I wait for the future.

We live in a free world,
Oh I am so excited.
Run to the future.
Live life to the maximum,
Die any time, any day.

Faith and what the future holds for me.
Open your heart to
Reality and imagination.

The world could end any time.
Have fun
Every day, life packed with new wonderful things.

Football is the future.
Unusual world
The nature and pollution.
Us for the future.
Running wild and free.
Everywhere I go, I see you smiling
                back at me.

Imran Khan (10)

DO YOU KNOW?

Did you know?
That 10% of flowering plants in the world are threatened with
extinction because we have damaged their natural habitat?
Or that acid rain from Britain, France and Germany is damaging
forests and poisoning lakes in Scandinavia?
And that one person living in Britain consumes the same amount
of the world's resources as forty poor people living in North Africa,
or even that all supplies of oil and natural gas will be
consumed by 2050?
So did you know any of these facts?
No, I didn't think so,
And, as one great man said . . .
'The world has enough for every man's needs, not every man's greed.'
I mean what have we done to our world?
What will happen to our world?
Why must we treat it like this?
If only I knew.

David Fisher (13)

The Rainforest

The birds are chirping in the trees,
The hyenas are laughing from ear to ear.
The cheetah is running in the cool breeze.
The parrots are playing along with the deer.
The monkeys are jumping from tree to tree,
The tiger is smug and full of glee.

The grass is green,
The stream is pure,
The trees are lean,
And it's for you to endure.

But how long for?
Nobody knows,
When this open door,
Will be shut, closed.

Charlette Hinds (14)

A WORLD FOR THE FUTURE

Humans are very dominating,
Think they can rule the world
without the consent of wildlife
and nature.

If only animals could
speak and we communicate.
But then again who's listening
and who's got the time?

It's only a minority who will
have the capacity to fight
with all their might, who will try to achieve anything
and something.

It will be too late,
Everything destroyed and distorted,
Everybody's remorseful for one's wrongdoing
And not blaming their own actions.

How about this world for the future?

Afshan Badshah

A World For The Future

The air contains pollution,
The ozone bears a hole.
Our stupid, selfish carelessness,
Has finally taken its toll.

We've all played our part,
However big or small.
Our stupid, selfish carelessness,
Has ruined it for all.

But do not fear there is still hope,
The candle is still burning.
To repair the delicate circle of life,
To keep that circle turning.

Oliver Lee (10)

THE FUTURE

In the future lots of fun,
And children playing in the sun.
Bees go whizzing all about,
Getting nectar from flowers that come out.
No more fighting, no more war,
We won't want to fight anymore,
There won't be pollution anywhere,
And more people will care.
Dancing bears have to be banned,
All that's allowed is to let them stand.
So in the future things may be better and sweet,
And you can talk to anybody that you meet.

Kitty Isaac (10)

NEITHER GOOD NOR BAD

Planet Earth.
A world of happiness and pleasure struggles
in competition with misery and hatred.
A paradise land with big, fat chimneys
Exhaling generous quantities of poison in
Disguise as thick, grey smoke which clashes
Beside the ultramarine sky.
Numerous roads interrupt the lush colour of
The natural green fields with the bland greyness.
'I was here first,' says the field in a language
Undiscovered by man.
'I am here now and soon I shall be in every
Space which was once occupied by you.'
Was the diabolical answer of the road.
Eventually, this natural world will be completely
Transformed into an unnatural dull planet.
And the natural roundness will pass into oblivion
As duplicate blocks and squares, the ragged
Grey buildings, will assume control.
The cause is man and his money.
One day, even money may overrule pollution and
A different competition will evolve between *them*.
I am human and they are human, yet I cannot
Understand their reluctance to reduce this effect.
But I cannot spend *all* my life worrying about this,
For I will not live to see the most shameful
Results of pollution and neither will the careless
People who started it.

Helen Withington (14)

A Waste Of Time

The year is two thousand and twenty,
Lots of people . . . but robots plenty.
Humans relax, are idle all day,
No time for work, just hours for play.
Robots have become the faithful slaves,
They are the plumbers, teachers and knaves,
Programmed to build houses tall and strong,
To drive all the trains narrow and long.
But this luxurious way of living,
With people taking, never giving,
Makes them selfish - I hope not like you.
Let's pray this vision never comes true.

Laura Eastwood (12)

WHAT'S SO DIFFERENT ABOUT GIRLS

I don't understand why boys complain about girls
when they whisper and snigger

But

what we don't realise is we do the same

Boys always say girls can't play football

But

most of them can and a lot of us can't
Girls always say their cooking is best

But

When us boys all get A's, they just don't know what to say

Adidas, Puma, Nike are the trend
That's what we all spend our money on

When we realise we are the same
Then all our lives won't be such a pain
So what's so different about *Girls?*

Antony Longmire (12)

GIRLS VS BOYS

One day they love you,
Next you're hated.
What goes on in their minds?

Who's at the bottom?
Who's at the top?
Of the Premier League of course!

Where are my trousers?
Where are my socks?
In his room, where else?

Just think what would happen,
With girls on the field
They'd have their hands in the sink!

Shelley Wood

GIRLS I DON'T KNOW WHY

Girls are sexist,
Girls are shy,
Girls are stupid,
and I don't know why.

Girls are tall,
Girls are small,
Girls hate football,
and I don't know why.

Girls are nasty,
Girls are grim,
Girls are bad losers,

And they hate it when you win!

Anthony Driver (13)

BOYS ON GIRLS

Girls can be decent,
Girls can be scruffs,
Girls can be posh,
Girls can be rough,
Girls can be nasty,
Girls can be nice,
Girls can be good-looking
Especially Baby Spice.

Simon Adams (13)

GIRLS ON BOYS!

Boys are so annoying,
Though some can be quite nice.
All they do is football and think about
'N-Tyce'.

My brothers are really horrible,
They tease me everyday.
They are so annoying,
I wish they'd keep away.

Boys are mainly horrible,
Though some of them are nice.
My brothers are really horrible,
They, are as cold as ice!

I wish that boys could be more 'gentle'.
They could be as nice as a choc-ice,
If, they really tried!

Annika Holliland (14)

A World For The Future

The world's cared and it's helped us
and fed us with its food
But, we've just used and cut it up
'Now look, there's nothing else to do'

The seas aren't grey, they're black now
with no fish to swim around
The dirt has piled high now
with no hope to see about

The bits of forests that there were
have totally all gone now
No sign of trees or life around
all burnt right down
The birds have all died out now
and insects have all been killed
No pandas or antelopes to wander through the hills.

The air is dark and misty
so thick and full of dirt
Nothing can be said now, 'cause it can't get any worse
A world that they said could get better,
better than it was,
Is nothing but a mere dream,
'cause there's no one left but me now!

Sukhveer Bhaker (13)

OUR FUTURE

Are we so blind that we cannot see,
What we are doing to you and to me.
The silence was golden until trees fell,
The earth has become a living hell.
We're polluting our seas and polluting the air,
But what we must ask, is do we care?
We must pull together,
And work as a team,
However difficult it may seem.
We can do it if we try,
And make a smile from a sigh.

Letty Lamdin

A World For The Future

There are different things that form the earth,
The trees, the fields, the hills and birds.
But if these all left without a trace,
And left behind the human race.
Then how great would our earth be,
Without the rocks, the cliffs and sea?
All this despair could come true.
Without the help of me and you.
Save the earth, the desert sand,
Let's make a change, you know we can!

Emma Swift (12)

PAIRAIR THE FUTURE

We share this world upon we are,
With a fellow, distant, far
You see me one, but one of Par
Is one of the relatives of the great 'Shar'.

He lives in a deep booming lair,
Under the ground of a planet called Pairair
But he is sad, sad for us,
His crystal tears decline and shatter,
While we above, carry on to patter.

He controls your life
Your way of living,
The grass of glass
The clouds so cunning,
The sea of serrated razor blades
Slicing his bitterness away.

He wounds our hearts, fears and tears
Looking through you see him peer,
Whisper straight back through that ear
'Our unborn life will soon be here!'

Sarah Morris (13)

CHILDREN IN CONFLICT

Children in conflict
We don't want to get involved
Whether a problem within the family
We just want to get it solved.

There all types of conflict
Within yourself or between a friend
We just hope sooner or later
It will all come to an end.

There are other types of conflict
Like bullying in school
The bullies try to embarrass you
So you look a fool.

There have been children in conflict
All over the world
The deaths of the Irish children
The innocent boys and girls.

So I conclude that conflict
Is a very tough case
I wish I could make it disappear
From the entire human race.

Michael Godwin (12)

FUTURE OF POLLUTION

We chuck our cans on the floor
We don't care anymore.
The dustbin-man does his job
We are just one lazy slob.
We now fight pollution a gruesome war
Pollution's winning what's the score.
It's spreading itself around
Oh no, another forest fell to the ground.
The clouds bustle up to send their acid rain.
The CFC's will not be merciful,
More holes they will make
When shall we wake.

Who is feeding this monster.
Why us of course.
With a can of drink on the floor
A packet of crisps and more.
They lay there, still on the ground,
Making a stink all around.
So now you shall stop and think hard
Are we cool or dying lard.
That can't be bothered to use a bin
Don't say no, it is a sin.

Jennifer Rickard (12)

TECHNOLOGY TIME-BOMB

The peaceful earth, which once people knew, is now a place of
                                                technology and ridicule,
People survived long ago and far away, without all this machinery day
                                                             by day.
So tell me why, or what has changed to people in this world today?
Is it we're selfish and greedy for more? Or are we ignoring the earth
                                                             so tore.
So carry on mindlessly - it's all fun and games.
It's your descendants, who'll pay the price and our excuses are lame.

Lindsay Hudson

STOP

What are we doing, can't we see?
This great big world was made for you and me.

When is it going to stop?
We simply can't go on
Killing and polluting simply just aren't on!

We have endangered species
but no one seems to care
Panda, tiger, elephant, extinction everywhere.

We must stop all this horror
before it gets too late.
Love and care for Mother Earth
before love turns to hate.

We must do something now,
before it gets too late.
Chopping down our trees
will surely seal our fate.

Rachel Laming (15)

LIKES

Girls like clothes, bags and shoes,
Boys like football, computers and fake dog poos,

Boys like lie-ins on a Saturday morn,
Girls like study, yawn, yawn, yawn,

Girls like a friend they don't like a stranger,
Boys like cars, bikes and danger,

Boys like computer games and lots of fun,
Girls like lazing in the sun,

Girls like Barbie, Sindy and dolls,
Boys like scoring lots of goals,

Boys like TV and electrical appliances,
Girls like maths, English and sciences,

Girls like glasses, cups and mugs,
Boys like spiders, insects and bugs,

Boys like boy things, girls like girls,
Let's just keep them in separate worlds.

James Bunning (12)

UNTITLED

Why do boys play at guitar?
Burp and think it's funny?
Always mess about and have a laugh?
And never save their money.

Why do boys channel surf?
And always have fake fights?
They think it'll impress us, but it never works
It's just a horrid sight

Why do boys act really hard?
It doesn't really suit them
Boys are soft like a lump of lard
So we should just ignore 'em.

Why do boys pull funny faces,
Try to be really rough,
Always talk in weird voices,
Can't they see we've had enough.

But all in all, boys are great
Us girls couldn't live without them
We treat them like mates
And get along in tandem.

Naomi Connor

BOYS WILL BE BOYS

Boys can be intelligent
Boys can be sweet
Boys can be pathetic
Boys can be weak.

Boys can be loud
Boys can be heard
Boys can be athletic and willing to learn

Boys can be entertaining
Boys can make you laugh
Boys can be clowns and boys can never get enough

Boys can be dangerous and are always quick to the blame
Boys send Valentine cards and anonymously sign their name?

Rachel Burbridge

MEN, BOYS, IDIOTS

Men, boys, idiots.
They're all of similar looks
They love football, food and computer games
Whereas we normally prefer shopping, talking and books.

Men, boys, idiots.
We'll take the men first.
Overgrown boys, that's all they are, they have matured at last
The only difference is their drinking, anything to quench their thirst

Men, boys, idiots.
Now for the boys.
They think they're great with their cars and diggers
But they're really just little boys with their toys

Men, boys, idiots.
They haven't a titter of wit
Summed up in one word,
It has to be . . . *idiot!*

Fiona Patterson

Boys

Boys can be fine
they can laugh
they can whine
boys can be great only by half.

Boys can be handsome
some can be charming
others can be gruesome
and even alarming.

From mud-pies
to footie kits
from telling lies
to battling their wits

From boys to men
they grow up fast
and that is when love comes at last.

Gemma Keith (12)

GIRLS ON BOYS

They're great,
They're nice,
They're sexy,
They're cool,

They're cute,
They're kind,
They're fun,
They're fine,

They're loveable,
They're romantic,
They're intelligent,
They're caring.

It's just a shame that from the above list
Only a few boys like this do actually exist!

Claire Hancock (14)

BOYS HAVE NO BRAINS

Fighting
fighting
every day
getting into trouble
in every way
never kind
never nice.
There are exceptions
but I think twice
they're always rough
and they all think they're tough.
Mummy's boy
daddy's boy
playing with a toy
after a while they begin to annoy.
Fidget here
fidget there
fidget, fidget everywhere
(Happens every day)

Holly Barton (12)

GIRLS ON BOYS

Will Smith, Adam Rickett,
David Schwimmer, Brad Pitt.
Will Mellor, Matt Le Blanc,
Leo Di Caprio, Tom Hanks,
Paul Nicholls, Matt Perry,
Nick Carter, Nick Berry.
Chris O'Donnell, Robbie Williams,
David Beckham, Jason Simmons.
Ben Freeman, Tim Hargreeves,
Jessi Spencer, Keanu Reeves,
Lee Brennan, Alex James,
Matt Damon, Dean Cain.
Jeremy Edwards, Darren Day,
I don't think there's much else to say!

Hannah Osborn (13)

Boys

Boys show-off and try to be tough,
Boys can be rude and very rough.
Boys can be kind,
Boys can be charming,
Boys can be shallow, caring, alarming.
Boys can be strong,
Boys can be weak,
Boys can be soft,
Boys can be sweet,
Boys can be slow, but fast on their feet.
Boys can be clowns,
Boys can be funny,
Boys make me laugh,
Boys make me cry,
Boys find it hard to be honest!
I don't know why?
Boys should say how they really feel,
Telling the truth is no big deal.

Karina Heslewood

GIRLS ON BOYS

Boys are weird,
It's the only way to describe them,
They act so pathetic and childish,
Surely they can never become men?

Boys are sad and rude and horrid,
They must be from another planet,
They stink and live like dirty pigs,
They should all be dumped in a huge, big pit.

I heard once or twice there's a partner for everyone,
That everyone has a perfect soul-mate,
I cannot believe there's someone for me,
Frankly, most boys I've met, I have to say I hate!

Caroline Ayres

WHAT WILL THERE BE?

I am no longer in this world.
No grass for me to feel,
No lingering breath in my lungs,
No sweet taste held in my mouth.
Now I am no more,
The people have changed,
New fashions,
New lives,
New destinies
In this time
The animals are now silent
New species have evolved.
But the beauty in the world,
Made by the animals,
Has gone!
The air held a clean, fresh fragrance,
But does no more
Disease and illness thrives
How?
Pollution!
The sky was once crystal blue,
But now filled with dirt and disease.
The waters were once blue,
But now are dank and dark.
Why?
Us!
Why did we leave such a world?
Where people in the future would have to live!
A world for the future,
Is now a jail for the innocent.

Abigail Watkins

EARTH

Round and round it twirls in space
with the sun gazing at it with a big, happy face,
Around it goes spinning again,
A new day has just begun.

So big, so round, so beautifully done.
But if we don't help now,
It will soon be gone.
Pollution here, killing there,
poverty and disease everywhere.

Gazing up very high.
Pointing to somewhere beyond the sky.
As I point I see a star.
From the earth it was very far

Time is wasting for the earth.
Everything dying, rotting to the ground.
Could there be a chance for a new birth?
A birth that's so big it could save the earth.
But up to now nothing's found
Looks like we're all going underground.

Ffion Haf Hughes (14)

THE WORLD

Where will the world boldly go?
Without land, sea or snow,
Will the wind still blow?
Not one person will ever know!

We'll walk at the wink of a toe,
We'll smile at the click of a doh,
We'll skip at the stitch of a sew,
That's what I think not know!

And when all the lights have been switched off,
We'll be falling free,
We'll have a feeling of inspiration and our ability!

Louisa Gibb (12)

NO ME... NO YOU

Now is the time
The time to fear,
The smell of death
Is uncomfortably near.
The world's getting old
So dirty too,
Some time in the future
There'll be no me . . . no you.

All it takes is for you to see
That the world needs help from us,
Take time to look, take time to notice
You don't need to cause a fuss.

The world needs help
So do the animals too,
Or else some time in the future
There'll be no me . . . no you.

Zoe Mitchell (16)

A World For The Future

Pollution is the worst,
Soon the earth is going to burst,
We need this to stop,
Or we will all go pop,
And if this carries on,
What will happen to your daughter or your son,
Think about the future!

Emma Deakin (12)

HOLD ON

It hurts to hear the sadness in your voice,
When you cry out in pain.
It hurts me to know you're losing the will to live,
The hurt drives me insane.

It kills me to see the position you're in,
The clock ticks by, it's late.
But keep on fighting with what energy is left,
It'll kill to lose you to fate.

It cuts deep to know you won't be here forever,
Guiding me through life.
It'll cut deep when life takes you away from me,
Cut deep, with a cold hearted knife.

But I know there'll be a place, where I can go to see you,
I know in my heart there's a place.
My memories will show me a picture of you,
And no tubes, just a smile on your face.

But whilst you're still here I'm taking advantage,
I'm gonna hold you ever so tight.
I apologise now, if you feel that I never let go,
I'm holding on with all of my might.

It pleases me to look really deep into your eyes,
They tell your life and all you have done.
It pleases me Gran to know that you're here,
So for me and your family *hold on.*

Victoria Whewell (16)

Boys

People say that boys are lucky
They can get all wet and mucky.
They can fight and climb up trees.
They do not cry when they scratch
                               their knees
They run away from us Miss's
Because they do not like our kisses
People say that boys are lucky
But I think that they're very
Yucky.

Cally Fitzsimmons

WALK ON BY

When I saw you for the first time.
I felt like jumping with glee,
I felt church bells ringing me.

I did not have the courage in me.
To go over and say, 'Will you go out with me.'
So I took a deep breathe and went and asked her.

She said, 'Yes,' I jumped with glee,
Then she said, 'Only joking, now go away
And stop bugging me.'

My heart was broken.
I was really sad,
Oh why, oh why, did you have to walk on by.

Michael McQueen

Nin 1901-1996

Even though we're
Far apart
Your memory will be forever
In my heart.

There were times when you
Were oh so funny
With your cotton wool hair
And monopoly money

With your friendly flair
And subtle talk
Your mischievious smile
And feeble walk

Your warm loving touch
Your Irish way
Your words of wisdom
Soon began to fray

You flew like a bird
To set yourself free
Away from the pain
But also me

I've asked myself why
So many times
But I can never find
No answers, no replies

The number of questions
Which taunt my mind
The answers, I wish
I could find

Are you a diamond
Of the night?
Sparkling down
And shedding your light?

Are you a flower
That blooms in May?
In the wind
So you gently sway?

Are you a pebble
That lives in the deep?
Embedded in the sand
So you softly sleep?

I'll leave these questions
Until we meet again
So goodbye
Until then
Rest in peace
Amen

Michelle McDonald

Why?

Why do we destroy this world of ours?
Why chop down the trees and flowers?
Why neglect wildlife that has done us no harm?
Why not live in peace and calm?

Why pollute the planet and all of life?
Why cause mother nature trouble and strife?
Why do we threaten our freedom to live?
Why not help others by learning to give?

Why is justice never rightly done?
Why have, so often, the criminals won?
Why is this planet laden with hatred and war?
Why aren't the rich treated the same as the poor?

Do we really care for our suffering world
Or is it cursed with decay
Can we protect it and keep it safe
Or is mankind's abuse here to stay?

Amanda Hampson (13)

A World For The Future

The world is full of love,
The world is full of hate,
The world is full of guilt,
And apologies which are too late.

The world is a funny place to live,
The world is very strange.
If I was in charge of the world,
Many things I would change.

There would be no more wars or fighting,
Not one bomb or gun.
Lots of people would find out,
That the world could be fun.

No more killing animals,
Not one cut down tree.
No more of anything cruel,
That's how it should be.

No more country rivalry,
No more of anything bad.
Because the way that the world works,
Is really quite sad.

The world should be a happy place,
Like a happy love filled heart.
But if the wars could only stop,
Then that would be a start.

Claire Nicole Pomphrett (13)

TODAY WAS NOT

Today was not,
very warm,
not very cold,
not very dry,
not very wet.
No one round here,
went to the moon,
or launched a ship,
or danced in the street.
There were no flags,
no songs,
no cakes,
no drums.
I didn't see any marches,
no one gave a speech.

Marie Simpson (11)

A World For The Future

A world for the future?
Who knows
How long it will be
Before it goes?

We're protected from the sun by the ozone layer,
If we carry on in this way, it soon won't be there,
Landfill sites, tyre dumps and nuclear waste,
It's time we changed our ways, and with haste!

If given the choice of riding a bike,
Or going on a country hike,
It would seem we would rather get in the car,
With effortless travel to near and far.

People seem to have no fear
That in twenty years time we may not be here.
Driving our cars with their terrible pollution,
We need an environmental revolution!

One day we'll be sat eating our dinner
Saying, 'So what if the ozone layer's getting thinner?'
When *Bang!* There is a terrible noise!
Where the earth once stood is a great big void.

Amy Lawrence (14)

A World For The Future

She is swift, relaxing, cool and refreshing
She caresses our faces and kisses us tenderly.
Yet we darken her classic features with fumes and smoke.
Air will fall and crumble to dust, nothing.
Earth is warm, tender-hearted and soft.
She is beaten down upon by her bright, fiery mother, the sun.

Motherly, caring to our race.
So why do we abuse earth with waste?
Water is clear and young, fresh and new.
So why do we make her ill, with our disgusting waste?

Filthy chemicals, rubbish, fumes,
Water shall die.
Care for the elements, care for nature.
Care for our mother sun
And her lover, the moon,
The air, earth, water and all creatures,
We will then create a beautiful world for the future.

Lauren C Argent (13)

BOYS, BOYS AND MORE BOYS!

Boys, boys and more boys,
They're nothing but trouble.
They just make fun of what you are wearing,
Or just say ' You're ugly or fat.'
But what would they know?
I hate boys, I wish that the whole world
Just consisted of girls,
Anything, but boys!

Emma Freeman (12)

I Don't Know How

It was then when I saw you, you said 'Hello.'
It was time to go home, but I didn't want to go.
Your eyes lit up like the sun in the sky,
So I just turned around and said 'Hi.'

It was then when I saw you, I began to stir,
It was then when I kissed you, I just didn't care.
I loved you then, I love you now,
I let you go, but I don't know how.

Sharon Arnold (12)

HE'S THE ONLY ONE FOR ME

He's the only one for me
The lad sitting next to me
He looks at me I turn away
My friends say, 'Do you think he's OK?'

He's the only one for me
The lad sitting opposite me
I think he's sound as a pound
Now you see he's the love I found.

He's the only one for me
The lad sitting in front of me
I look at him he looks at me
And now I'm down on one knee.

He's the only one for me
The lad standing next to me
He smells so funny but looks so nice
Why can't you go out with me tonight?

He's the only one for me
The lad standing opposite me
I look and smile for a while
Now you see he's in my smile.

Tanya Bailey (12)

A World For The Future

There's too many cars
The pollution's high
And the factories pour out smog
People drop litter
And kill all the animals.

People get killed by passing cars
They go too bloomin' fast
50, 60, 70, 80,
The speed just keeps going up.

Dogs go to the loo up the lampposts
They should have a dedicated field
You never know what's on your feet
So be careful where you tread.

Go to work in the morning,
But don't come back in the evening
Pollution *stop it!*

Rob Lean (13)

THE TURNING OF THE CENTURY

I sat and thought about the Millennium today,
Of what we will do
and what we will say.
The old ones among us
will recall the good times and bad
The younger ones just a good time to be had!

Should we throw a party?
And bury a tube
filled with memories, and wishes and wine.
Where will we be,
in just five hundred days
Possibly a million miles away.

'For I have a dream'
(If you'll pardon the pun)
of being the first on the Earth
To witness in all its glory
the land's rebirth.
Oh I know there'll be pilots
in outer space.
Oh I know there'll be one
or two
But let me tell you
right here and now,
I'll be among the lucky few
to herald the advent of not just
a brand new day
but a new life for me and for you.

Vicki Hancock-Ekberg (13)

A World For The Future

When we jump into the car
do we realise what pollution we are causing?
Or just that old sweet-wrapper that we throw on the floor.

Do we think about the problems we are causing the environment
because we'd better start thinking soon
or we will have no wildlife or country parks left.

The pollution that the power stations let off is awful,
no wonder there is global warming.
I think we should do something about it and make our stand now.

Christopher Thompstone

A World For The Future

In the future she will be a much better world to live in.
In the future she will under go international cosmetic surgery.
Every nation will be in debt to her beauty, for they were the
cause of her deep scolding wounds.
In the future she will be renowned for her grace of peace by
her eight brothers and sisters,
As no more battles need to be fought,
For there is no more blood to be shed.
In the future she will show her true feelings,
No more will she lie asleep listening to the cries of hunger and deceit.
In the future she will be admired by each race,
Sharing her love and nourishing her children as a mother,
Covering her rounded figure with a security blanket.
In the future she will be a much better world to live in.

Annabel Stevenson (13)

A World For The Future

I'm looking over a city
But it's covered in smog
People can't breathe properly
What if the world dies?

Lorries rush past,
Their noisy horns are annoying,
Taking waste to the dump,
Burying it in the ground.

The sea is turning green,
The fish are all dying.
Over-fishing them won't help,
Soon the sea will be dead.

We should stop polluting,
Go out and recycle more,
Use your cars less,
Make the world a better place.

Michael Connolly

HERE COMES THE MILLENNIUM

There is a big event coming to town,
Everyone have a party.
This talk of a new beginning,
They called it the millennium.

The millennium will change the world,
It will be a new start for mankind,
The millennium should bring peace between one another,
So we can live in harmony.

The new start should bring joy
But also will bring hope for the less fortunate.
This event is not all good,
But at the time nothing will matter to anyone
but only the millennium.

There are more big events that also affects the world,
This event is passionate to all the people.
The event is called the World Cup.
These two events are both times of importance to the world,
Remember the millennium will only happen once in our lifetime.

Paul Chandler (13)

THE RIGHT ROAD

The year 2000 lies ahead of us,
It is our future.
Everything could change,
A dream car could turn into a solar-powered car.
An alien could land on Earth, and be our friend.
Our lives could change,
We could travel in time,
Medicines will improve,
Our homes will change.
They may consist of nothing but a computer,
They may consist of everything but a computer.
We never know what may be ahead of us.
It could be a dark and lonely path.
It could be a path with dazzling bright lights.
You just don't know.

Nicola Farrer

TOMORROW

Twenty years from now, at this time
There'll be a record fall in rates of crime,

> *One in five children get asthma today,*
> *Tomorrow it'll be one in five who don't.*

We'll be calmer, have more control in our lives,
We can lie back and feel the economy thrive.

> *Single currency in a single language-speaking world*
> *Will kill all conversation.*

No more bad behaviour, nor disciplinary hearings,
That'll all be stopped by genetic engineering.

> *No news, just data processing,*
> *No friendships, laughter or acts of human kindness.*

Twenty years may seem ages to sit and wait,
But it shouldn't be long now, they've set a date.

> *So a warning, I issue to you. Don't forget what you gave*
> *up when you're sitting in your man-made, empty life, doing nothing.*

Lizzie Harvey (17)

THE MORNING OF TOMORROW

A watery sun rises above the sleepy world,
Casting long, black shadows across the ragged grass,
All begins to awaken and stir,
As a fox scuttles across the carpet of dew.

A river gurgles over pebbles of paint,
Twinkling in the early sunlight,
A bird begins to sing a golden song,
As flowers open their petals in the heat.

A cool breeze rustles the leaves,
And an aroma of flowers fills the air,
Spots of colours dance in the fields,
The gentle music of the wind.

Underneath the dark green hedgerow,
There lies a tangle of roots and soil,
A white dove flies overhead,
The only movement in the wide open sky.

The crow of a cockerel in a nearby farm,
Announces the bright new day,
The countryside bursts into action,
To welcome the incoming morning.

Tine Berg (12)

A World For The Future

The ozone layer is in a mess
The snow of the Antarctic is becoming less
Trees are being continuously cut down
Which leaves certain animals wearing an angry frown.

Animals are being killed for their ivory and skins,
Hunters are committing horrible sins,
Foxes are running because they're being chased.
These people of their own medicine they need a taste.

People are living on the streets
They can't even afford little treats.
Both children and adults are being treated badly,
So are animals, this is the truth, sadly.

The world shall be a wreck in years to come,
If us, the people don't get something done.
Unborn children will have totally missed
Sharks, tigers and other animals which no longer exist.

We all have enemies in our minds
Though the worst in the world is mankind.

Zoë Thompson (13)

A World For The Future

If pollution keeps on happening,
And if we keep polluting all the streams,
Soon all wildlife and all plant life,
Will all be in our dreams.

The waste in the water,
Kills the animals in the sea,
And the pollution in the air,
Can kill you and me.

The air will be thick and black,
There'll be stumps instead of trees,
There'll be the drone of chain saws,
Instead of the drone of bees.

We must stop all the pollution,
We must do something fast,
We must stop pumping smoke into the air,
Or nothing on Earth will last.

We must stop destroying plant life,
We must stop polluting air,
We need to grow more plants and trees,
And all kinds of flowers that are rare.

If we want our children to grow up healthy,
And if we want a nice clean Earth,
We must stop pollution right this minute,
And remember what our Earth is worth.

Catherine Phillips (13)

A WORLD FOR THE FUTURE

Down down down we go
Wildlife goes down with us
Bit by bit it's disappearing
'Cos of hunters, factories and human beings.

Factories are poisoning our lovely environment
Goes into the oxygen into the air
How can we breathe with so much poison
People just don't seem to care.

What is happening to our lovely nature
Homes being built where flowers used to grow
No more glowing in the summer sun
What will we do when they're all gone.

I wish this world was full of love
Peace and harmony too
All the flowers you can think of and pretty colours too
With birds flying, rabbits hopping free
That's how we should be
With love in our hearts to share around
That's how people should be.
With fresh air for our children to breathe
No cars no factories to poison our air
I could do it so why can't you
My future world would be where people love, care and share.

Faye Willicott (14)

Our World In The Future

How do you see our world of the future?
As one big Millennium dome?
Bursting at the seams with technology beyond our comprehension?

Or will it be like today, only made more convenient,
never having to even leave your home?

Will the world be full of riots, war and death,
Or peace throughout all nations, countries and races?

Will we still have a need for people, as friends and family for companionship and love,
Or will computers provide all the friendship we need?

Will global warming be so immense that we will be living in a tropical climate?

We can't answer these questions, nor can anyone.

Only time can tell us, only time.

Charlotte Marshall (13)

INFORMATION

We hope you have enjoyed reading this book - and that you will continue to enjoy it in the coming years.

If you like reading and writing poetry drop us a line, or give us a call, and we'll send you a free information pack.

Write to :-
**Triumph House Information
1-2 Wainman Road
Woodston
Peterborough
PE2 7BU
(01733) 230749**